DK SUPER History

CALIFORNIA GOLD RUSH

Discover the excitement, chaos and tragedies of the gold rush that transformed California in the 1800s

PRODUCED FOR DK BY
Editorial Just Content Limited
Design Studio Noel

Author Marissa Moss

Senior Editor Ankita Awasthi Tröger
Editor Hattie Hansford
Senior Art Editor Gilda Pacitti
Graphic Story Illustrator Matt Garbutt
Managing Editor Carine Tracanelli
Managing Art Editor Sarah Corcoran
Pre-Production Coordinator Shanker Prasad
Pre-Production Designer Jaypal Chauhan
Production Controller Rebecca Parton
Publisher Sarah Forbes
Managing Director, Learning Hilary Fine

First published in Great Britain in 2025 by
Dorling Kindersley Limited
20 Vauxhall Bridge Road,
London SW1V 2SA

The authorised representative in the EEA is
Dorling Kindersley Verlag GmbH. Arnulfstr. 124,
80636 Munich, Germany

10 9 8 7 6 5 4 3 2 1
001–350118–Sep/2025

A CIP catalogue record for this book
is available from the British Library.
ISBN: 978-0-2417-4475-8

Printed and bound in China

www.dk.com

This book was made with Forest Stewardship Council™ certified paper – one small step in DK's commitment to a sustainable future.
Learn more at www.dk.com/uk/information/sustainability

Contents

Words in **bold** are explained in the glossary on page 44.

History in Perspective

On 24 January 1848, a **carpenter** named James Marshall noticed something shiny in a river in California. It was gold! This discovery started a **phenomenon** known as the California gold rush. People from all over the world raced to California, hoping to find gold and get rich.

Where and when?

The gold rush happened in California, which was not yet a state. It was a territory that the United States had forcibly taken from Mexico, following a **brutal** war. The rush for gold started in 1848 and lasted until about 1855. During this short period, California changed a lot.

Who was involved?

The gold rush attracted lots of people who left their homes and travelled to California in search of riches. **Miners**, who were mostly young men, were nicknamed "forty-niners" because they arrived in 1849. People from as far away as China, Chile and Mexico came over hoping to make their fortune. **Merchants** also set up in California to sell supplies – they often made more money selling **shovels** and **pans** than the miners made finding gold.

Indigenous peoples had lived in California for thousands of years before the start of the gold rush. The sudden arrival of miners and settlers brought violence and disease to their communities. Many were forced from their ancestral lands. By 1870, about 80 per cent of Indigenous individuals who had once lived in California had either died or been forced to move away.

New settlers looking for wealth claimed much of the land in California. They built towns for their families and set up shops to sell supplies.

California was a peaceful place before the gold rush. It was home to several Indigenous communities, each with their own ways of life and traditions.

Different perspectives

Different groups in society may have deeply contrasting experiences of events. Official records of the past often only present one side of the story. This means that they can't reflect the experiences of everyone affected. To understand what happened, it is important that we look at events from more than one point of view.

Think about it

What kinds of **sources** could we use to learn about the gold rush?

Marshall first discovered gold in a river next to Sutter's Mill in California.

Key Events

WHAT HAPPENED WHEN

The 1848 gold rush changed California forever. Thousands of people travelled there, hoping to make their fortune. It was a time of excitement and adventure for many, but it also brought great **hardship** and loss for Indigenous communities.

1846

APRIL

The Mexican-American War starts when the United States takes Texas from Mexico, and the two countries can't agree on where the border is. The US wants to move west to get more land, like California. Fighting begins in the area they both claim, and the US declares war.

1847

13 JANUARY

Mexican and American forces sign the Treaty of Cahuenga. The **treaty** stops the fighting and gives control of California to the US military.

1848

24 JANUARY

James Marshall finds gold at Sutter's Mill in California. His discovery marks the start of the gold rush.

2 FEBRUARY

The US and Mexico sign the Treaty of Guadalupe Hidalgo. This treaty officially ends the Mexican–American War. The US pays Mexico $15 million. In return, Mexico gives California, New Mexico, Utah, Nevada, Arizona, Texas, some of Wyoming and most of Colorado to the US.

AUGUST

Word spreads that there is gold in California. Around 4,000 miners head there in search of their fortune.

5 DECEMBER

In his **State of the Union** address, the US president James K Polk announces that gold has been found at Sutter's Mill.

1849

Thousands of people known as "forty-niners" rush to California to find gold. This leads to violence against Indigenous communities. Many white settlers, including miners and **vigilantes**, attack Indigenous villages, forcing people from their homes.

1850

9 SEPTEMBER

California becomes the 31st state of the US.

1851

The California state government allows different groups – such as miners, **mercenaries** and the US Army – to remove Indigenous peoples from their ancestral homelands. Thousands of Indigenous individuals are killed or forced to leave.

1853

Hydraulic mining is introduced to California by American inventor Edward Matteson. The technology becomes popular as it helps miners dig deeper for gold. Powerful water jets wash away surface dirt and rock, making it easier to find gold that is hidden deep in the ground.

1855

Miners struggle to find any more gold. Many leave California, but some stay to search in new areas.

Key People
WHO'S WHO

The California gold rush was a major event that changed a lot of people's lives. Some found gold and became rich. Others faced hard times and suffered greatly because of it. In addition to the thousands of forty-niners, here are some of the key people in this story.

John Sutter

Businesspeople

John Sutter
A fur trader who built Sutter's Fort and Sutter's Mill, where gold was found. His property was stolen by **prospectors** during the gold rush, leaving him with almost nothing.

Sam Brannan
A **Mormon** leader who arrived in San Francisco by ship in 1846 and helped a group of Mormons settle there. He sold supplies to miners and became California's first **millionaire**.

Luzena Stanley Wilson
A woman who became rich during the gold rush by running businesses like a hotel and a restaurant for miners.

Sam Brannan

President James K Polk

Politicians

President James K Polk

The US president at the time that gold was discovered in California. He made the discovery famous by talking about it during his State of the Union address.

Governor Peter Burnett

The first **elected** governor of California. He wanted to make laws to stop Black American people from living in California. He also supported harmful actions against Indigenous communities, such as forcing them from their land. His ideas were unpopular, and he resigned after one year.

Explorers and discoverers

James Marshall

A carpenter who discovered gold at Sutter's Mill. He hoped to make money by partnering with John Sutter, but he never became rich.

James Beckwourth

A formerly **enslaved** man who became an explorer once he gained his freedom. He found a path through the Sierra Nevada, making it easier for people to get across the mountains to California.

James Marshall

Key Location
BODIE MINING TOWN

When prospectors first arrived in California, they lived in tents and makeshift shelters. Over time, more permanent houses were built, mostly using wood from local forests. The **settlements** were often given unusual names such as Whiskeytown, Drunkard's Bar and Angel's Camp.

One famous example was Bodie Town, located north-east of Yosemite Park. It was named after WS Bodey, who travelled from New York and found gold there in 1859. Sadly, Bodey died the same year in a snowstorm. But people kept coming there to look for gold. It is estimated that by 1890 Bodie Town had 2,000 houses and a population of almost 10,000 people.

The peak years of the gold rush lasted from 1849 to 1855, but mining continued for many years afterwards. After 1890, gold became much harder to find, and some of the mining companies were **bankrupt**. Many people moved elsewhere. In 1892, a fire destroyed most of the west of Bodie Town. Another fire in 1932 burnt down most of the buildings, but some survived and still stand today.

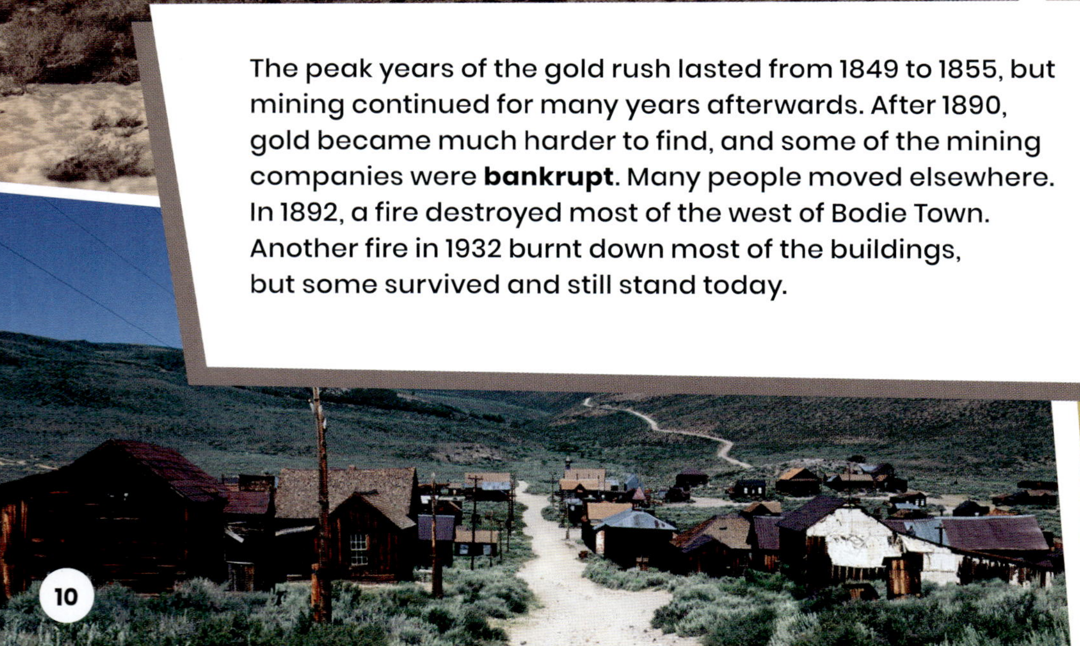

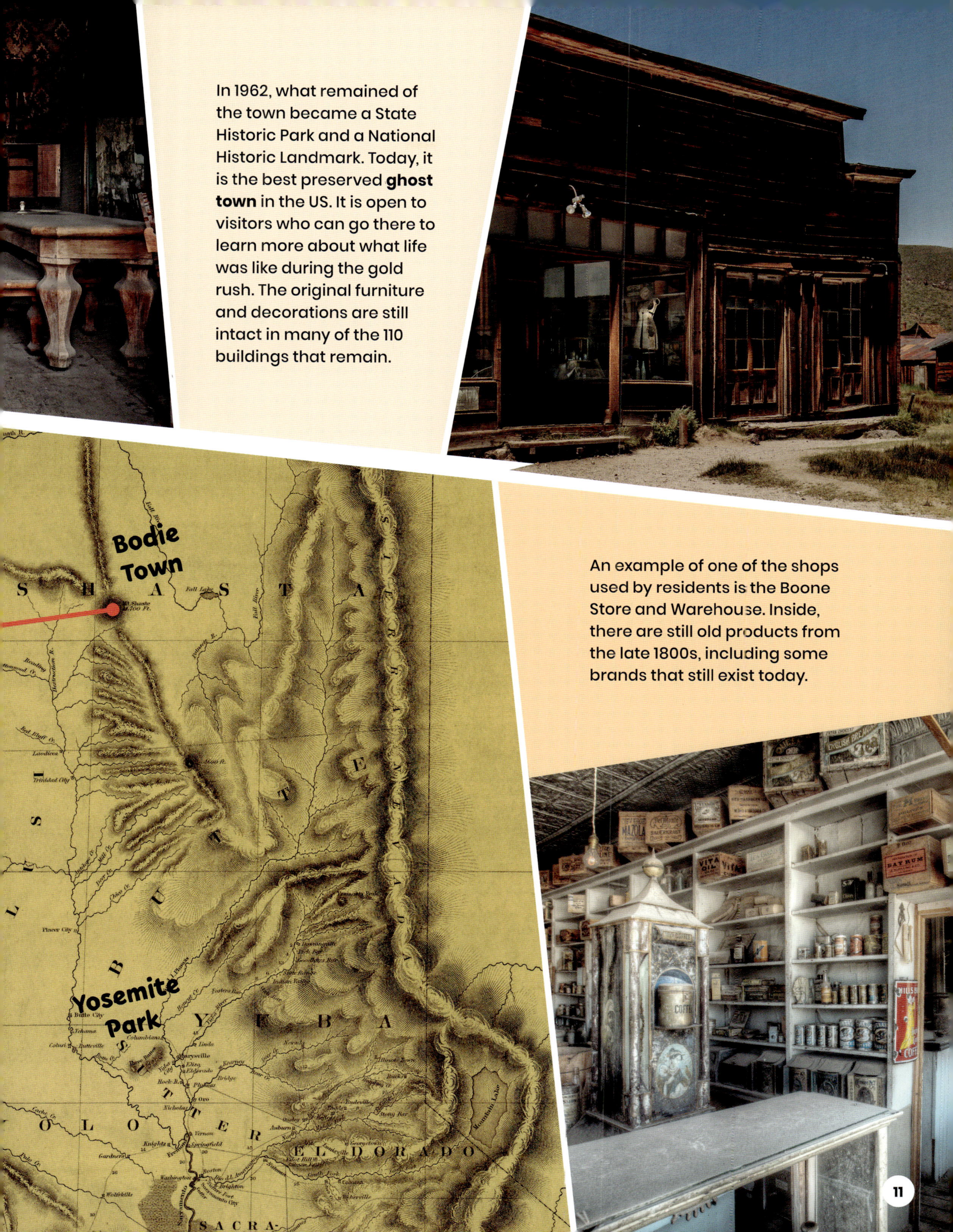

In 1962, what remained of the town became a State Historic Park and a National Historic Landmark. Today, it is the best preserved **ghost town** in the US. It is open to visitors who can go there to learn more about what life was like during the gold rush. The original furniture and decorations are still intact in many of the 110 buildings that remain.

An example of one of the shops used by residents is the Boone Store and Warehouse. Inside, there are still old products from the late 1800s, including some brands that still exist today.

New Arrivals

The region that is now California was home to many different groups of Indigenous people who had been living there long before anyone else arrived. It had been their home for thousands of years and they knew the land very well. They had their own languages, ways of living and traditions. But with the arrival of new groups of settlers from other parts of America, Mexico and Spain, conflicts arose and things began to change.

UNDER MEXICAN RULE

When Mexico became its own country in 1821, it included California. California was sparsely populated with rolling hills and thick forests. It was far away from the busy East Coast, where many Americans lived.

THE ARRIVAL OF THE SPANISH

From the late 1700s until 1834, Spanish explorers arrived in California. They set up **missions** to spread their way of life and the Catholic religion among local populations. This led to many forced **conversions**, the spread of diseases and the loss of Indigenous cultures.

Spanish explorers built places called missions, like this one, throughout California.

Sutter, pictured here in his thirties, moved to California in 1839. He wanted to build a settlement. So, he asked the Mexican governor for a big piece of land by the Sacramento River.

JOHN SUTTER'S DREAM

John Sutter was a fur trader who came to California from Switzerland, looking for new opportunities. His dream was to create a place in the countryside where people could live and work together. He built a settlement known as Sutter's Fort in 1839, in what is now Sacramento, the capital of California.

Think about it

How did Mexican control and the arrival of the Spanish explorers and American settlers affect Indigenous communities?

THE MEXICAN–AMERICAN WAR

During the Mexican–American War, which lasted from 1846 to 1848, the United States took control of California. Once the war ended, American settlers worked to develop the area. Sutter built a settlement called New Helvetia. He helped many Americans move to California. He also worked with Mexican leaders and American settlers to help the region grow.

Sutter's Fort was a busy centre used for farming and trading.

Striking Gold

James Marshall worked as a carpenter at Sutter's Mill. On 24 January 1848, just a few days before the end of the Mexican–American War, he spotted something shiny in the river. He looked closer and wondered if he had found gold. Excited, he asked some other workers to come and see. Little did they know that this moment would eventually lead to the dramatic events that soon followed.

After Marshall found gold, people heard the rumours and came to investigate. What they saw amazed them – gold that they could pick up by the handful!

Marshall found gold in the river next to Sutter's Mill.

AN IMPOSSIBLE SECRET

Four days later, Marshall told his **boss**, John Sutter, about his find. Sutter worried that greedy people would come and ruin his land. He tried to keep the news a secret, but the workers already knew. Sutter decided to let his workers search for gold on their days off, as long as they did their job on their work days.

Thousands of people came to mine for gold near Sutter's Mill.

GOLD! GOLD!

Samuel Brannan, a Mormon leader, businessman and journalist, moved to California in 1846. In 1848, he heard about gold being found at Sutter's Mill. Brannan saw a chance to make money. He bought tools for mining and opened a shop near where the gold was found. To get people excited and to buy from his shop, Brannan did something clever. He ran through San Francisco holding a jar of gold. He shouted about the gold discovery so that lots of people heard about it. His newspaper, the *California Star*, also helped spread the word.

The news about the gold travelled around the world. Marshall's discovery inspired many people to come to California to find gold and get rich. By the summer of 1848, about 5,000 men were mining for gold near Sutter's Fort.

Brannan told everyone he could about the gold at Sutter's Mill.

Fascinating fact

The first American gold rush started in North Carolina in 1799.

In 1848, gold was worth as much as $35 per ounce. In today's money, that would be about £900 per 25 g.

Word Spreads

News of the gold at Sutter's Mill did not spread as fast as it would today. Most people in the United States lived thousands of miles from California. The quickest way to spread news was by sea. In the summer of 1848, news reporters started writing about the gold. Richard Mason was the **military governor** of California. He sent a report along with some gold all the way to Washington, DC.

Governor Richard Mason sent gold to Washington, DC. It helped confirm that the discovery was real and not just a rumour.

Steamships like this one helped transport news far and wide.

EXCITEMENT BUILDS

Miners were constantly finding lots of gold. This made people very excited. By the summer of 1848, people were hurrying to California from places like Hawaii, Mexico, Chile, Peru and China to look for gold.

THE PRESIDENT'S SPEECH

The excitement peaked on 5 December 1848. This is when President James K Polk mentioned the gold discovery during his State of the Union address. He said the gold mines were probably bigger and more valuable than anyone predicted.

Fascinating fact

Before the California gold rush, only royalty and the rich owned gold mines. So when Marshall found gold in 1848, it was like a huge treasure chest had opened. People from all over the world raced to California, hoping to find gold too.

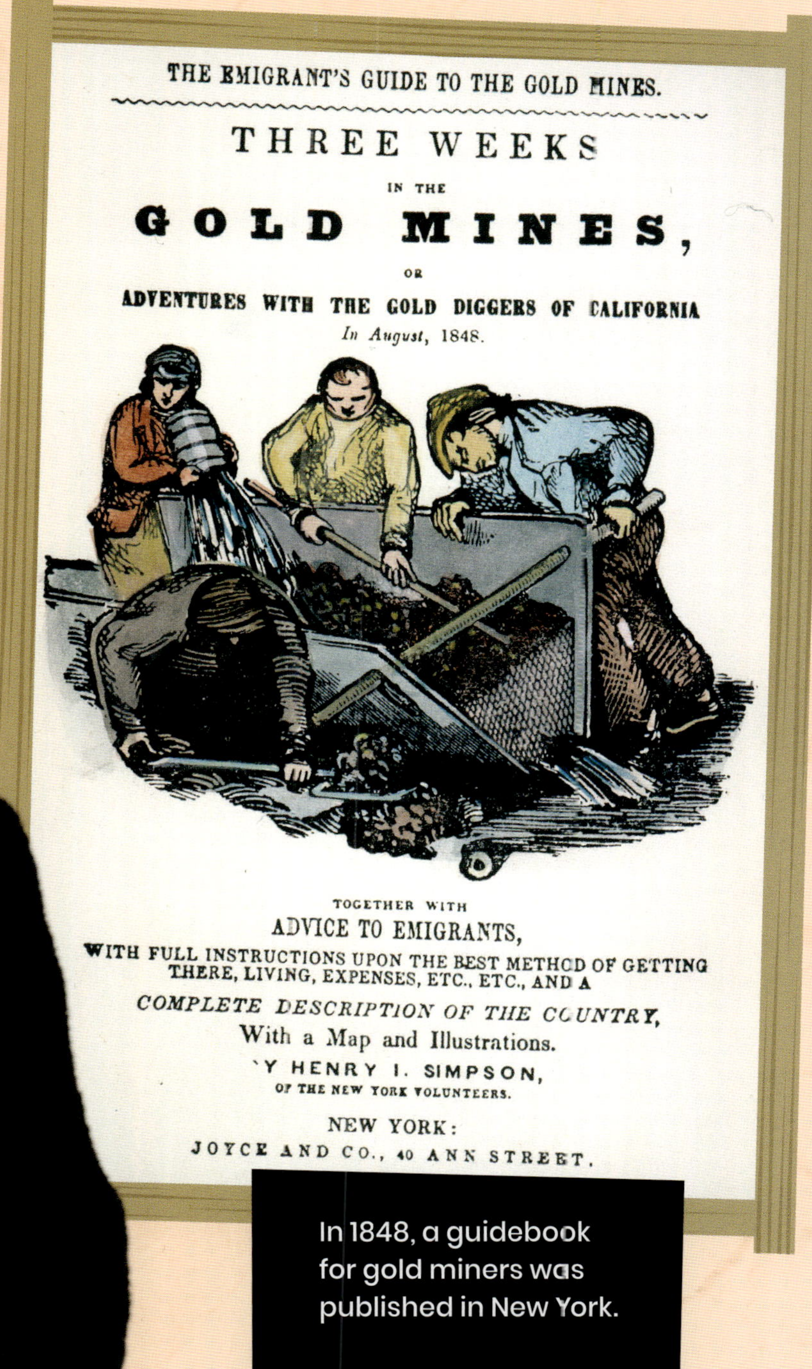

THE EMIGRANT'S GUIDE TO THE GOLD MINES.

THREE WEEKS

IN THE

GOLD MINES,

OR

ADVENTURES WITH THE GOLD DIGGERS OF CALIFORNIA

In August, 1848.

TOGETHER WITH

ADVICE TO EMIGRANTS,

WITH FULL INSTRUCTIONS UPON THE BEST METHOD OF GETTING THERE, LIVING, EXPENSES, ETC., ETC., AND A

COMPLETE DESCRIPTION OF THE COUNTRY,

With a Map and Illustrations.

`Y HENRY I. SIMPSON,

OF THE NEW YORK VOLUNTEERS.

NEW YORK:

JOYCE AND CO., 40 ANN STREET.

In 1848, a guidebook for gold miners was published in New York.

President James K Polk

Journey to California

The California gold rush began when news of the gold spread across the United States and the world. Many people dreamed of finding riches, but first they needed to get there. Back then, travelling to California was very different from today.

FOR CALIFORNIA.

French's Express Passenger TRAIN.

From NEW YORK to Port LAVACA, in Texas, by Steamship, thence by comfortable and
easy wagon coaches along the line of our military post, through San Antonio, Western Texas, El Paso,
and the gap of the Sierra Mimbres mountains, near a place known on the common maps as San Diego,
in New Mexico, along the southern bank of the Gila, for nearly four hundred miles, thence north-west
over its waters and those of the Colorado, along the margin of the coast range of mountains, to San
Francisco.
This route crosses the Continent in the mild regions of the 29° and 30° N. L., ascending gradually
over the gently swelling uplands of Western Texas, through the delightful and cultivated country around
El Paso, where the U. S. troops are now stationed, down the banks of the Gila, amid the ancient Aztec
ruins, and hieroglyphic evidences of a civilization that has long since passed away, thence over the
magnificent plains of California to San Francisco.
To the hardy and adventurous, of whatever nation, but especially to the excitement loving people of
our own country, this route has charms that no other possesses; but were we to add to the mild climate,
the excitements of camp life, the chase, and the ever varying scenery, the all powerful charm of gold, the
incentives are complete. That gold does exist in great abundance along the course of the Gila, is the
conviction of all that have passed over this route; and from some wonderful rumors that have been
whispered about of late, the well informed are of opinion that the tide of emigration will soon pour
into this region equal to the Sacramento Valley. That there are rich gold mines there, we have the
old Spanish authorities for the fact.
Thirty large spring coach wagons have been prepared, drawn by six mules each—spare mules, together with cattle, accompanying the expedition, for its use. Good tents, camp stools, water breaks,
portable stoves, portable boats, and everything necessary for the expedition, have been amply prepared.
The Company will be divided into messes, each mess to be provided with a Cook. The ser-
vices of an experienced Physician has been engaged. Sixty Texas Rangers, well mounted, accompanying the expedition as an escort, to hunt and scour the country by day, and stand guard by night, accom-
panied by two mountain howitzers and experienced guides, the whole under the command of Capt. Charles
Naylor, who served during the Mexican war with great gallantry.
A corps of Topographical Engineers will accompany us; in fact, the Company will enjoy all the
facilities that government can render.
Those going to California will do well to call and examine the plan. The provisions consist of
bacon, bread, coffee, sugar, and such wild game as may be killed by the way. We will leave New
York 25th of April.
Price of passage $250. Each passenger allowed six cubit feet of baggage. For passage or par-

Wagon companies started advertising trips to California.

TRAVELLING BY WAGON

Some people travelled across the country by wagon. For safety, they often travelled in groups or caravans called wagon trains. These wagons were pulled by oxen or mules and could carry families with children. Travelling overland could take months.

DEALING WITH DANGER

Travelling by wagon was cheaper, but it was dangerous. There were risks of accidents, as well as attacks from wild animals. Diseases were common along the route, and lots of people became ill and even died.

These paintings depict groups of travellers heading to California in wagons and on foot.

TRAVELLING BY SEA

For prospectors travelling west from the eastern or central US, the trip could take weeks or even months. The safest – but slowest and most expensive – sea route was sailing around Cape Horn at the southern tip of South America. The journey took about six months and stretched over 18,000 **nautical miles**.

Another option was to sail to Panama in Central America, trek through the jungle, and then board a ship heading to California. This path was shorter. It cut off about 12,875 km (8,000 miles) and saved months of travel compared to the Cape Horn route. But it was not easy. Travellers faced tropical diseases like **yellow fever** and **malaria**.

Travellers often faced storms and sickness along the way.

By the time travellers arrived in California, they were very tired from the long journey.

ARRIVING IN SAN FRANCISCO

Many gold seekers arrived by ship from places such as Mexico, Peru and China. When they reached San Francisco, they found a small town. Yet it was on its way to becoming a bustling city full of miners, all eager to strike it rich.

Fascinating fact

During the California gold rush, more than 1,000 old ships were left behind along the coast of San Francisco. Over time, the water **receded** and the city was built on top. There are more than 70 ships buried under the streets today.

Gold Rush Pioneers

Luzena Stanley Wilson
A pioneer woman, originally from North Carolina

Mason Wilson
Luzena's husband, a farmer, originally from Missouri

Thomas and Jay Wilson
The children of Luzena and Mason Wilson

Pioneers
People who moved to California, hoping to find gold

Gold miners
People who mined for gold, also known as forty-niners

After months of crossing vast plains, high mountains and scorching desert, the family arrived in California.
The goldfields were teeming with prospectors from around the world, all hoping to make their fortune.
Ma'am, I'll give you $10 for some of that. I haven't eaten good food in so long.
Panning for gold may not be the only way to make money here.
The family sold their oxen and bought a share of a hotel in Sacramento.
As more people came to mine for gold, business boomed for the family.
Hungry miners need good food as much as gold.

After weeks of rain, the new city flooded.
The levee's broke!

Our dreams are washed away. Where can we go now?

I heard they struck it rich in Nevada City. That's where I'm heading.
Maybe we could start again there.

It took twelve days over the mountains to reach the mining camp at Nevada City.

Luzena started again with the best way she knew to make money.
Hotel El Dorado

We are so busy, we need more cooks and waiters!

In 1851, a huge fire destroyed the wooden buildings of Nevada City, including the hotel.
Fire! Fire!
The fire left the Wilson family homeless and with only a few dollars.
We recovered before, and we'll do it again.
The family returned to a crime-ridden Sacramento.
We need somewhere a little quieter.
The family moved to Vaca Valley, away from the rough and rowdy gold rush towns.
Wilson's Hotel
My food is worth its weight in gold!
Wilson's Hotel
Where do you folks call home?
We've seen a few homes in gold country, but we'll be staying here for now.

Staking a Claim

At the beginning of the gold rush, many people thought finding gold would be easy. But searching for gold was very hard and often dangerous. Miners used tools like shovels and pickaxes to dig in the ground. They also had a special shallow pan with sloping sides to help them wash away dirt and gravel to find gold. Some miners even made their own tools, like cradles that rocked in the water to help separate the soil more easily.

Although miners had tools to help them, they needed to be strong to dig for many hours every day.

The demand for supplies was so high that merchants were able to sell them for a lot of money. For example, a pan that once cost 20 cents might be sold for $15 during the gold rush.

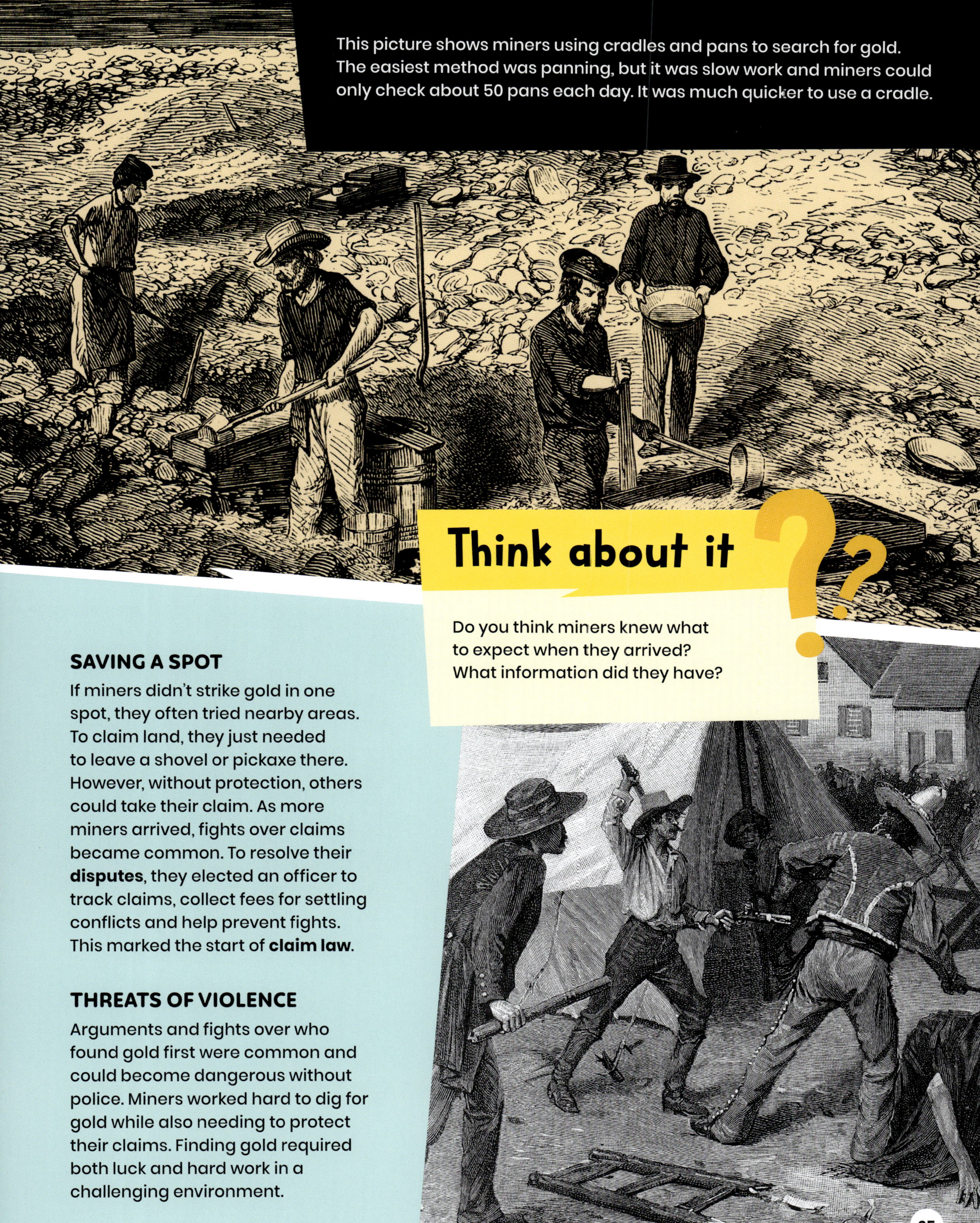

This picture shows miners using cradles and pans to search for gold. The easiest method was panning, but it was slow work and miners could only check about 50 pans each day. It was much quicker to use a cradle.

Think about it

Do you think miners knew what to expect when they arrived? What information did they have?

SAVING A SPOT

If miners didn't strike gold in one spot, they often tried nearby areas. To claim land, they just needed to leave a shovel or pickaxe there. However, without protection, others could take their claim. As more miners arrived, fights over claims became common. To resolve their **disputes**, they elected an officer to track claims, collect fees for settling conflicts and help prevent fights. This marked the start of **claim law**.

THREATS OF VIOLENCE

Arguments and fights over who found gold first were common and could become dangerous without police. Miners worked hard to dig for gold while also needing to protect their claims. Finding gold required both luck and hard work in a challenging environment.

Life as a Forty-Niner

The forty-niners got this name because so many of them went to California to look for gold in 1849. When they finally got there, most ended up living in poor conditions in small, dirty camps or tents. Even though life was hard, they kept working because they hoped to find a lot of gold.

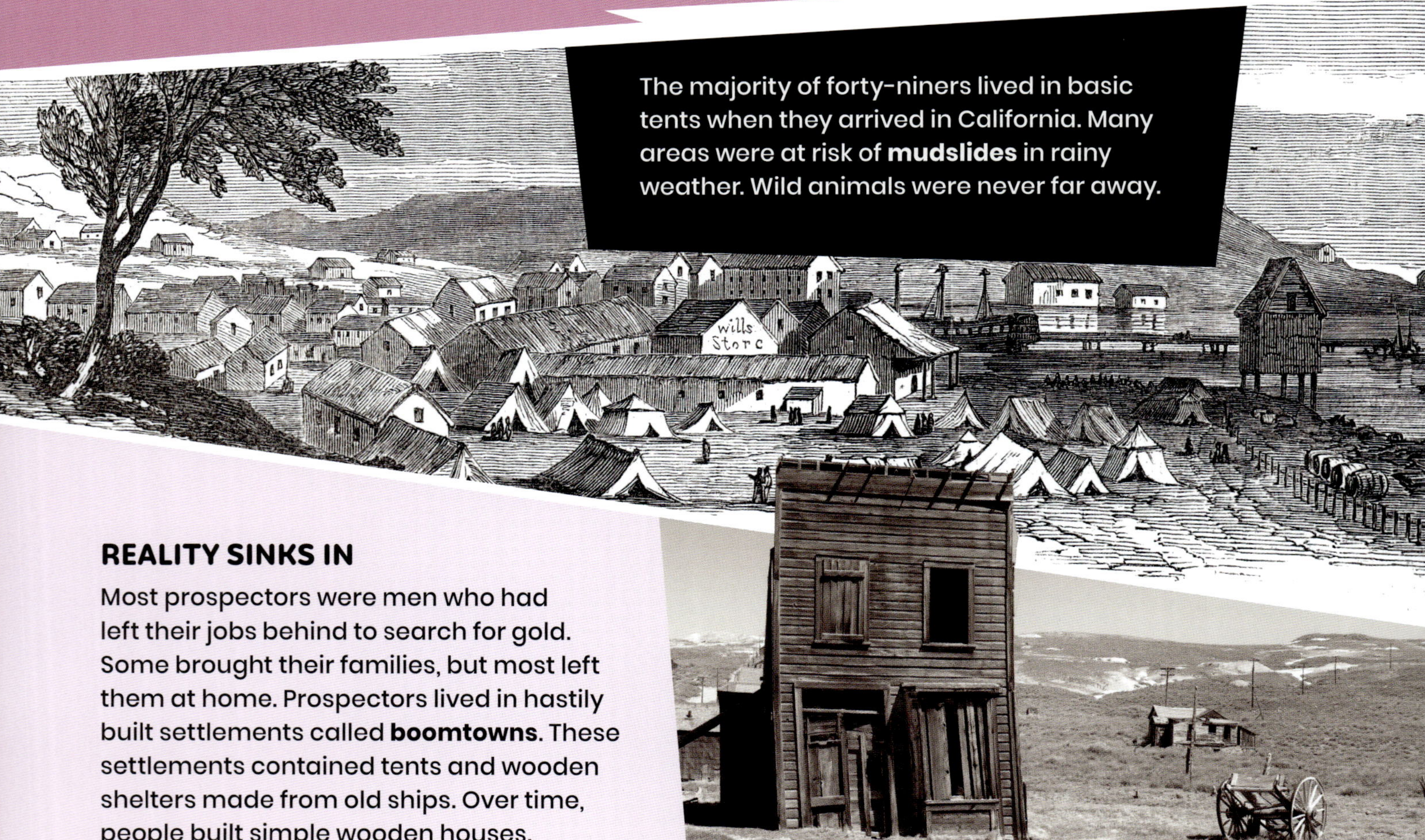

The majority of forty-niners lived in basic tents when they arrived in California. Many areas were at risk of **mudslides** in rainy weather. Wild animals were never far away.

REALITY SINKS IN

Most prospectors were men who had left their jobs behind to search for gold. Some brought their families, but most left them at home. Prospectors lived in hastily built settlements called **boomtowns**. These settlements contained tents and wooden shelters made from old ships. Over time, people built simple wooden houses. The boomtowns had no running water, making it hard for people to stay clean. This caused sickness to spread quickly.

Today, many of the gold rush boomtowns are empty and are known as ghost towns.

This painting shows a busy bar during the gold rush.

FREE TIME

Miners worked hard during the day but often spent their evenings drinking and **gambling**. Many were frustrated when they did not find gold, which sometimes led to fights in the towns. There was also a lot of racism and conflict among different groups of people.

FEMALE FORTY-NINERS

While most miners were men, women also played important roles during the gold rush. They earned money by cooking meals and washing clothes for miners, who paid well for food and comfort. Among these women were Luzena Wilson and Sarah Royce.

In 1849, Sarah travelled to California with her husband, Josiah. Their journey from Iowa was complicated and challenging – they even got lost in the desert. They arrived in October 1849, prospected for gold and opened a shop. Royce wrote about her experiences in a book called *A Frontier Lady*. Her story highlights the **resourcefulness** of many women during the gold rush.

Fascinating fact

Sometimes women disguised themselves as men in mining towns. One job advertisement asked no disguised women to apply.

The Golden State

CALIFORNIA BECOMES A STATE

California's journey to becoming a state was unusual. Most places had to be organised territories first, but California skipped that step. The gold rush played a big role in making California a state quickly. Gold was found in 1848, and by 1850, California was already a state. The whole process took less than three years, which was very fast.

By the end of 1849, about 100,000 people had arrived in California looking for gold. This number kept growing as many more people arrived over the next ten years. People came from all over the United States and around the world. This made California a **diverse** place with many different cultures.

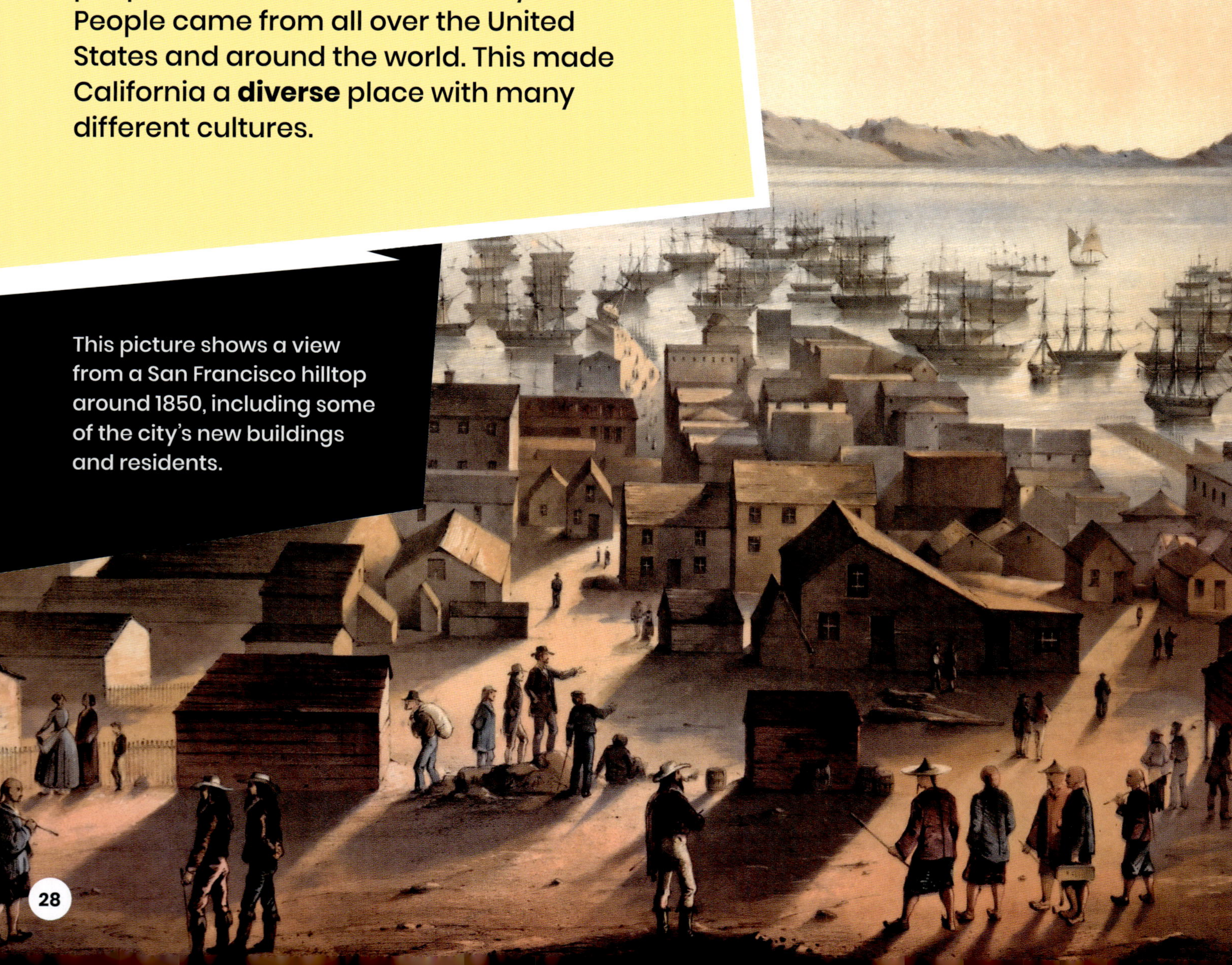

This picture shows a view from a San Francisco hilltop around 1850, including some of the city's new buildings and residents.

CALIFORNIA JOINS THE UNION

In 1849, a meeting was held in Monterey, California, to draft a **constitution**, and by the autumn of 1850, California officially became a part of the United States. San Jose was the capital of the new state from 1849 to 1851. The capital was then moved, eventually settling in Sacramento in 1852.

The state constitution was drafted at Colton Hall.

The excitement of the gold rush started to slow down by 1857. But some people continued to look for gold in California for many years after.

THE GROWTH OF SAN FRANCISCO

San Francisco quickly changed from a small town into a major **port** city. The population grew rapidly. It turned into a busy place with lots of opportunities for miners and shopkeepers. Before the gold rush, around 1,000 people lived in San Francisco. But by 1850, this number had increased to about 25,000. It became a major hub for those hoping to find gold.

Fascinating fact

Today, San Francisco is one of the most diverse cities in the US. People from many different races, ethnicities and cultures live there.

Crime and Violence

Day-to-day life in and around the **goldfields** was tough for many people. Crime, violence and **discrimination** were common. In the early days of the gold rush, there were no set rules and no police officers. This meant that miners had to protect themselves and solve their own problems. Everyone wanted to find gold. This led to lots of arguments and fights over who claimed the land.

Fights often continued away from the goldfields. Difficult, crowded living conditions and **drunkenness** made them worse.

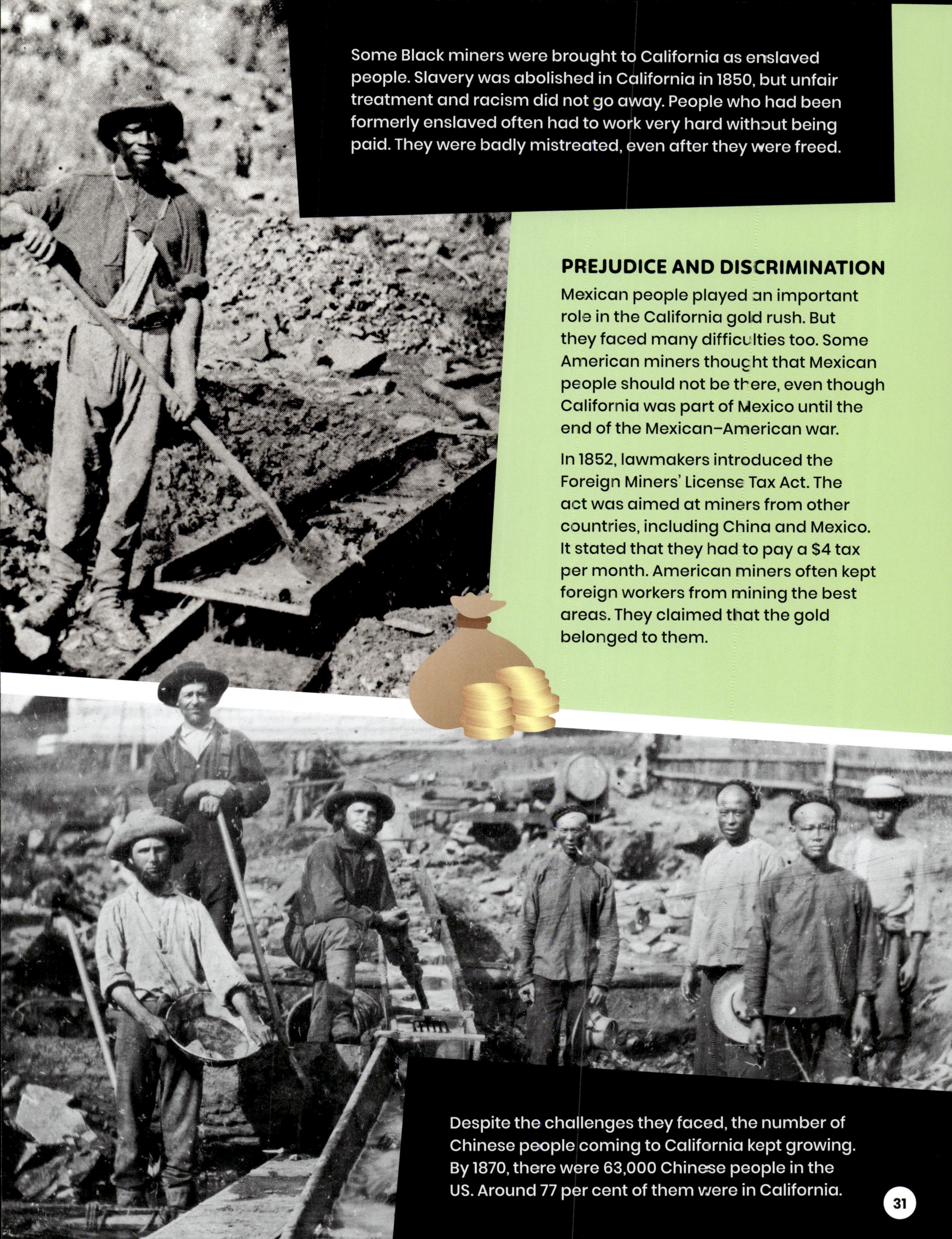

Some Black miners were brought to California as enslaved people. Slavery was abolished in California in 1850, but unfair treatment and racism did not go away. People who had been formerly enslaved often had to work very hard without being paid. They were badly mistreated, even after they were freed.

PREJUDICE AND DISCRIMINATION

Mexican people played an important role in the California gold rush. But they faced many difficulties too. Some American miners thought that Mexican people should not be there, even though California was part of Mexico until the end of the Mexican–American war.

In 1852, lawmakers introduced the Foreign Miners' License Tax Act. The act was aimed at miners from other countries, including China and Mexico. It stated that they had to pay a $4 tax per month. American miners often kept foreign workers from mining the best areas. They claimed that the gold belonged to them.

Despite the challenges they faced, the number of Chinese people coming to California kept growing. By 1870, there were 63,000 Chinese people in the US. Around 77 per cent of them were in California.

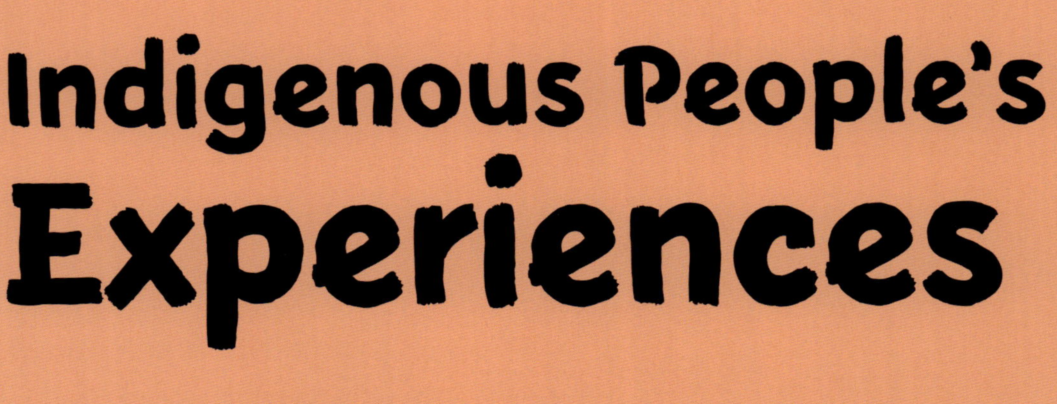

Indigenous People's Experiences

Before 1849, California was home to about 150,000 Indigenous people. It was also home to around 7,000 people of Spanish or Mexican descent – many were descendants of Spanish settlers, and some had both Indigenous and Spanish ancestors. But by 1855, more than 300,000 migrants had come to California, mostly from other parts of the US.

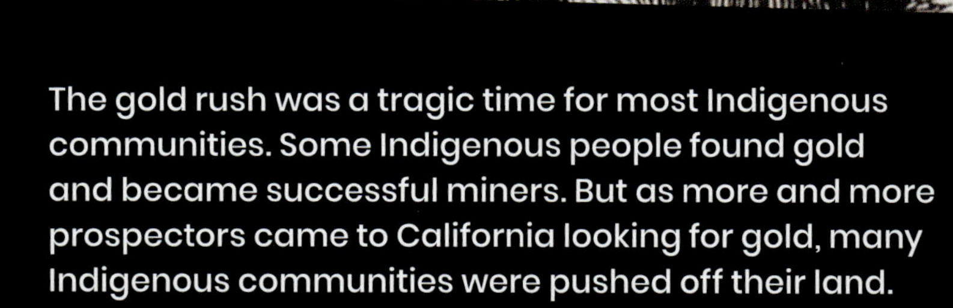

The gold rush was a tragic time for most Indigenous communities. Some Indigenous people found gold and became successful miners. But as more and more prospectors came to California looking for gold, many Indigenous communities were pushed off their land.

Think about it

Many gold rush stories leave out the impact on Indigenous peoples. Why do you think this is?

A BRUTAL LAW

In 1850, California governor Peter Burnett passed a law called the Act for Government and Protection of Indians. Under this law, Indigenous people could be arrested, forced into **hard labour** without pay, enslaved and even sold at **public auctions**. Indigenous children could be taken away from their parents and forced to work for strangers. They could not go back home. This brutal act destroyed many Indigenous families.

Peter Burnett

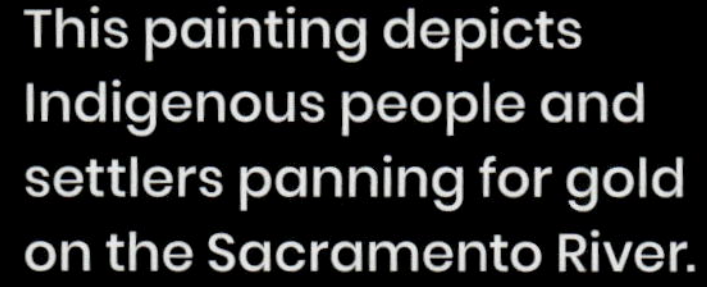

This painting depicts Indigenous people and settlers panning for gold on the Sacramento River.

NEW DISEASES

Europeans brought diseases that Indigenous people had never **encountered** before. This caused them to become very ill and even die. Many lost their homes. By the end of the gold rush, very few Indigenous communities were left in California.

Striking it Rich

When forty-niners left their jobs, homes and families, they all wanted one thing – to get rich. While some miners found a lot of gold, most of them faced gruelling work and needed expensive equipment. Many miners did not get rich at all.

Sam Brannan's shop made as much as $5,000 a day selling tools and equipment to miners. In today's money, that would be about £93,000.

THE FIRST MILLIONAIRE

Aside from finding gold, there was another way to get rich – selling to miners. At the height of the gold rush, an egg could cost as much as $25 (£20 in today's money). A pair of boots could cost thousands of dollars. Merchants would buy pans for just 20 cents and then sell them for $15. This meant that many Californian millionaires made their fortunes by selling people goods instead of mining for gold.

Sam Brannan opened a shop near the goldfields. It sold all the tools and supplies miners needed, such as shovels and pans. Brannan made so much money that he became California's first millionaire without ever mining for gold himself.

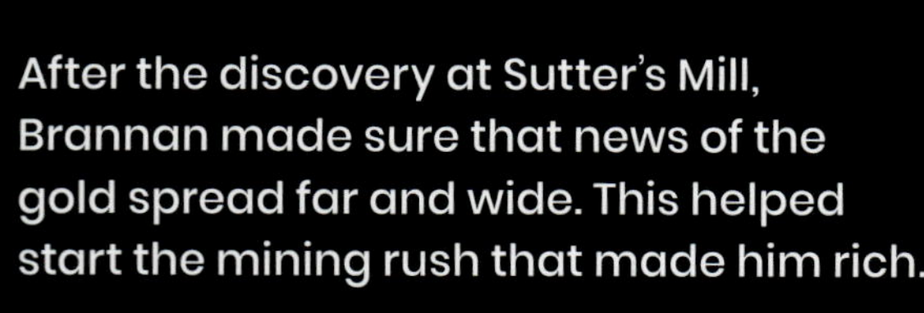

After the discovery at Sutter's Mill, Brannan made sure that news of the gold spread far and wide. This helped start the mining rush that made him rich.

James Beckwourth was known for telling stories of his adventures. He offered advice on the best path through the mountains to California.

GOLD RUSH ENTREPRENEURS

Beckwourth was born enslaved, but he gained his freedom at the age of 18. He became an explorer and businessman. In 1852, he opened a hotel in the Sierra Valley called the War Horse Ranch. The hotel offered food and lodgings to travellers.

Instead of mining, Levi Strauss sold supplies to miners. In 1853, he began selling rugged denim overalls for hard work. His business became very successful. Levi's® jeans are still sold today.

Beckwourth wrote a book called *The Life and Adventures of James P Beckwourth*. He was one of the only Black American people to have their life story published at the time.

Fascinating fact

While most of the miners did not get rich, the total amount of gold found in the gold rush would be worth more than £2.3 billion in today's money.

Gold at a Great Cost

Hydraulic mining used very strong water jets to break apart land and find gold deeper underground.

After 1850, mining changed a lot. Instead of individual miners searching for gold, big businesses took over a lot of the land. They introduced a new way of searching for gold using a method called hydraulic mining.

Fascinating fact

You can see a hydraulic mine in Grass Valley, California. It is in the foothills of the Sierra Nevada mountains. You can even pan for gold in the river there.

THE IMPACT ON NATURE

This new way of mining helped find more gold, but it was very bad for the environment. Miners blasted the land with water, creating huge amounts of **debris**. All this debris blocked up bodies of water, such as the Yuba and Feather Rivers. This led to flooding that destroyed farmland. Mining companies also cut down a lot of trees to make firewood and create open space.

Mining companies **polluted** the water and soil with **toxic** substances they used while mining.

MALAKOFF DIGGINS

Mining caused a lot of damage to nature at Malakoff Diggins in California's Sierra Nevada foothills. Miners used powerful water hoses to wash away entire hills, leaving a huge hole. This made the water in nearby creeks and rivers dirty and unsafe. Many plants and animals died because of the mining.

This picture shows hydraulic mining at Malakoff Diggins in 1871.

Judge Lorenzo Sawyer took two years to work out exactly how mining had damaged farmland.

Woodruff's lawsuit led to the first law to protect nature in California.

THE SAWYER DECISION

Many farmers were angry about the damage mining was causing to their land and waterways. In 1882, Edward Woodruff, a wheat farmer, **sued** one of the big mining companies — he wanted to stop farmland from being damaged. Two years later, Judge Lorenzo Sawyer gave a verdict limiting hydraulic mining. This was called the Sawyer Decision. But by then, most of the environmental damage had already been done.

Lessons from History

The gold rush changed California and the US forever. After the discovery of gold at Sutter's Mill, thousands of prospectors rushed there hoping to get rich. Some people benefitted and made their fortune, but some suffered greatly as a result. So why do we remember the California gold rush, and what can we learn from it?

THE EFFECT ON CALIFORNIA

The California gold rush turned places like San Francisco into busy cities. The rush for gold pushed the US to recognise California as a state, grew the economy and offered many business opportunities. It attracted people from all over the world. The impact of the gold rush can still be seen today – the state is one of the most diverse in the US and has the largest economy.

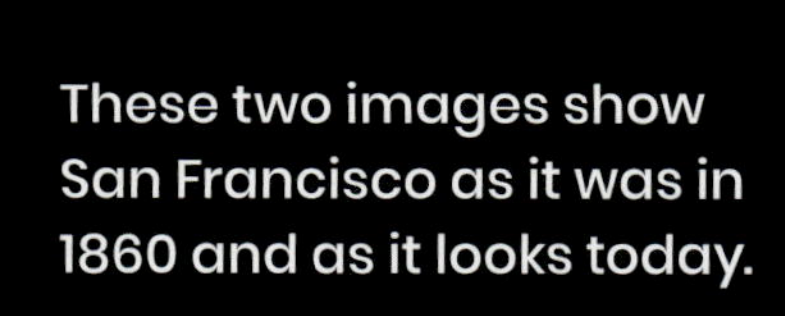

These two images show San Francisco as it was in 1860 and as it looks today.

This picture depicts an Indigenous community in Yuba. Their ancestors had lived in the region for thousands of years before settlers arrived. But as a result of the gold rush, many of these Indigenous groups were displaced.

THE NEGATIVE IMPACT OF THE GOLD RUSH

The gold rush was a terrible time for many people. Indigenous communities had lived in California for thousands of years. But they were forced off their land by new arrivals. Many became ill and died from new diseases they had never encountered. Families were torn apart as Indigenous individuals were sold and made to work for no pay. Many migrants experienced discrimination and racism, including miners from China and Mexico who faced unfair treatment and were made to pay extra taxes. The rush to get rich led to a lot of cruelty. The actions of big businesses also had a long-term impact on nature.

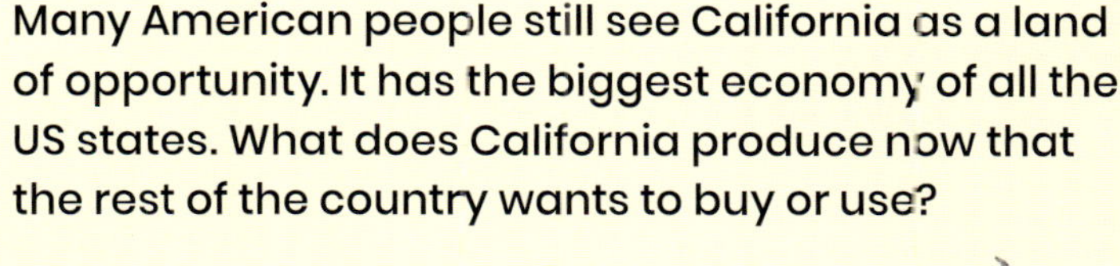

Think about it

Many American people still see California as a land of opportunity. It has the biggest economy of all the US states. What does California produce now that the rest of the country wants to buy or use?

PIONEERING SPIRIT

The gold rush tells a story of grit and determination. The forty-niners left their jobs, homes and often their families to try to build better lives for themselves. Prospectors risked their lives to travel thousands of miles, dealing with intense work and poor living conditions. The settlers who managed to stay on built communities and businesses that shaped California's future.

Uncovering the Truth

A lot is known about the people and events of the gold rush. This is because there are so many primary and secondary sources available. A primary source is a document or object created at the time of a historical event. A secondary source is a document or object created after the event, or by someone who was not directly involved in it. They can explain or interpret primary sources. They help in understanding an event.

Primary sources include

- official documents
- letters
- diaries
- paintings or drawings
- photographs
- sound recordings
- videos

Secondary sources include

- news articles
- books
- media documentaries
- encyclopaedias

Original photograph

DIFFERENT POINTS OF VIEW

Primary and secondary sources may tell different stories depending on the views of the people who created them. An Indigenous person who was forced from their land would have a different perspective from a prospector who found gold. It is important to question sources – doing this helps us to understand them and understand different perspectives better.

A PHOTOGRAPH

This photograph was taken around 1850. It is a primary source. It shows a man called Alonzo Doolittle standing next to a bag of gold. He was a **surveyor** who made maps of the goldfields.

Photo of original source

A PLAQUE

The oldest Chinese temple in Weaverville, California, has a plaque which was put up in 1980. It is a secondary source. The temple is called the Weaverville Joss House or the "Temple Amongst the Forest Beneath the Clouds". It was first built in 1853 and then rebuilt in 1874 after a fire destroyed the original building. The Weaverville Joss House was very important for Chinese culture and religion. The sign and the temple help us remember how Chinese immigrants were involved in the gold rush and the challenges they faced.

Original source text

Hundreds of Chinese miners came to the Weaverville area in the 1850s and prospered despite **hardships**, discrimination and tax on foreign miners. The first house of worship burned in 1873. The Chinese continued their religious traditions in the present temple, dedicated on April 18, 1874. Moon Lim Lee, trustee and grandson of one its contributors, gift-deeded the "Temple Amongst the Forest Beneath the Clouds" to the state.

Look at the photo and the plaque, then read the annotations and transcribed text and answer the questions below.

Quick questions

- Why were maps important in the gold rush?
- Why do you think Doolittle was photographed?
- Why is there a plaque to mark the Chinese temple?

Discussion questions

- Why do you think Doolittle was standing next to a bag of gold?
- What can we learn about the experience of Chinese miners from the plaque?
- Do these two sources tell different stories? Why do you think it's important to examine different sources?

- They helped people look in the best places to find gold.
- Surveyors were important during the gold rush.
- It remembers the Chinese immigrants during the gold rush and the challenges they faced.

Vocabulary Builder
Missing Home

What might a journal entry written by a miner in the California gold rush be like? Read this fictional diary entry to see how a lonely miner might express his thoughts. Pay attention to key words that describe how the miner is feeling.

15 December 1849

It has been three long months since I arrived here in California. Every morning I hope it will be my lucky day, but I always come back to this tent empty-handed, my whole body aching from working so hard all day. I miss my wife and my children more than anything. I promised them I would come back rich, but each day I lose faith that I ever will.

The rain hasn't stopped for days. I'm cold and hungry, but I spent all my money on a new pan because someone stole mine.

I watch as others find gold while I carry on digging through dirt with nothing to show for it. Everyone seems angry – there are arguments about whose spot is whose so I daren't leave my shovel. I'm worried about my safety and my future.

I often wonder whether this was all worth it. The dream of getting rich just isn't coming true. If things do not change soon, I fear I may have to turn back home, defeated, and with nothing to show for myself.

Imagine you are a forty-niner keeping a record of your life in California. Then use the diary entry on page 42 and the prompts and word bank below to write your own entry.

- **What was your day like?**
- **Have you been lucky or unlucky?**
- **How do you feel?**

Mining	digging, excavating, panning, sifting, sorting, washing
Living	cabin, camp, homesickness, illness, isolation, lawless, lean-to, physical danger, settlement, shelter, town
Feelings	angry, determined, disappointed, excited, hopeful, lonely, sad, scared, tired, upset

Glossary

Bankrupt When a person or business can't pay their debts and legally admits they do not have enough money to cover what they owe.

Boomtown A town that grows very quickly, usually because there are jobs nearby or valuable resources.

Boss A person who runs a business and has employees.

Brutal To be very harsh.

Carpenter A person who builds things using wood, such as furniture or houses.

Claim law As it relates to the gold rush, the laws for making mining claims.

Constitution The written laws that govern a country. The United States has separate constitutions for each state, in addition to the United States Constitution that applies to the entire country.

Conversion When people change their religion to follow a different religion.

Debris The pieces of something that has been destroyed or damaged, such as the rubbish or dirt left after a storm.

Discrimination Unfair treatment due to prejudice.

Dispute A disagreement between people or businesses. It may need to be resolved in court.

Diverse To have a lot of different things or people in one place.

Drunkenness The state a person is in when they have drunk too much alcohol.

Elected To be voted into office, such as a governor or president.

Encountered To have come across someone or something.

Enslaved To be forced to work for someone else without the freedom to stop or leave.

Gambling Playing games, such as card games, in order to win money.

Ghost town A once-prosperous town that has been quickly abandoned, leaving behind houses, buildings, and even personal possessions.

Goldfield An area where gold is found.

Hardship A difficult situation that makes life hard, such as being poor or having health problems.

Hard labour Very difficult work that is done by hand.

Hydraulic mining A form of mining that uses very strong jets of water to find minerals such as gold underground.

Indigenous Indigenous peoples are groups of people who are the original inhabitants of a region or area. There may be many different groups of Indigenous peoples within a region, each with their own languages and cultures.

Malaria A disease spread by mosquitoes that causes fever and chills. It was common in some areas during the gold rush.

Mercenaries Soldiers who fight for money instead of for their own country or beliefs.

Merchant Someone who buys and sells things as a job. Also known as trader or shopkeeper.

Military governor An elected official who governed California before it became a state.

Millionaire A person who has over one million dollars.

Miner A person who works to find valuable things, such as gold or coal.

Missions Places set up by Spanish explorers where people could learn about the Catholic religion and master new skills. They often led to the loss of local cultures.

Mormon A member of the Church of Jesus Christ of Latter-day Saints, a religion that was founded in the early 1800s in the United States.

Mudslide The dangerous slide of mud and dirt downhill due to heavy rain.

Nautical mile A unit of measurement used at sea that is longer than a normal mile. It helps sailors measure distances over water.

Pan A flat, shallow container used by miners to wash away dirt from rocks and soil in order to find gold.

Phenomenon A very important or unusual event.

Polluted To be harmed by the release of toxic substances. Often used to describe natural areas, such as land or bodies of water.

Port A place where ships can load and unload goods.

Prospector A person who searches for valuable minerals, especially gold, in the earth.

Public auctions Events where items are sold in front of an audience to the highest bidder. Historically, these also included the inhumane practice of selling enslaved people.

Receded To have moved backwards.

Resourcefulness The ability to solve problems or make things work with limited resources.

Settlement A community, such as a village, formed by people who have moved into a new area.

Shovel A tool with a broad blade used for digging or moving dirt and other materials.

Source A written document, artefact or building that provides information relating to the past. Sources are also known as evidence.

State of the Union An annual speech given by the president of the United States to tell people about how the country is doing and what its future plans are.

Sued To have taken legal action against someone or something. A person who is sued might need to go to court to resolve the dispute.

Surveyor A person who measures and maps out the land.

Toxic To be harmful to living things.

Treaty An official agreement between two or more groups, such as two countries, that states how they will act or what they will do.

Vigilantes People who take the law into their own hands to stop crime or punish wrongdoers. In the context of the gold rush, vigilantes often targeted and attacked Indigenous communities, using false claims of crime or wrongdoing as an excuse.

Yellow fever A disease spread by mosquitoes that can make people very sick. It was common in some areas during the gold rush.

Index

Acknowledgments

The publisher would like to thank the following for their kind permission to reproduce their photographs:

(Key: a-above; b-below/bottom; c-centre; f-far; l-left; r-right; t-top)

4-5 Alamy Stock Photo: YA / BOT (t). **5 Alamy Stock Photo:** Archive Images (tr); North Wind Picture Archives (br). **6 Alamy Stock Photo:** Everett Collection Historical (tr); World History Archive (c); Ivy Close Images (br). **7 Alamy Stock Photo:** FOST (bl); North Wind Picture Archives (tl); Niday Picture Library (tr). **8 Alamy Stock Photo:** North Wind Picture Archives (bl); The Picture Art Collection (cl). **9 Alamy Stock Photo:** Granger Historical Picture Archive (tl); North Wind Picture Archives (br). **10 Alamy Stock Photo:** Ian Paterson (bl). Courtesy Burton Frasher Collection. **10-11 Alamy Stock Photo:** Andrew Fare (b); Cristiano Montagnani (t). **11 Alamy Stock Photo:** Martin Williams (br). **12 Alamy Stock Photo:** ClassicStock. **13 Alamy Stock Photo:** North Wind Picture Archives (t); World History Archive (cl); Science History Images (br). **14 Alamy Stock Photo:** Lakeview Images (tr). **Getty Images:** Bettmann (bl). **15 Alamy Stock Photo:** (bl); North Wind Picture Archives (t); Granger Historical Picture Archive (br). **16 Alamy Stock Photo:** Old Paper Studios (b); PJF Military Collection (t). **17 Alamy Stock Photo:** Granger Historical Picture Archive (cr). **Bridgeman Images:** The Stapleton Collection (bl). **18 Alamy Stock Photo:** Yogi Black (t). **Bridgeman Images:** Look and Learn (b). **Getty Images:** MPI (c). **19 Alamy Stock Photo:** North Wind Picture Archives (b). **Getty Images:** Ullstein bild Dtl (t). **24 Alamy Stock Photo:** Danita Delimont (bl); Granger Historical Picture Archive (r). **25 Getty Images:** Ullstein bild Dtl (b); Universal Images Group (t). **26 Getty Images:** EyeJoy (br); Heritage Images (c). **27 Alamy Stock Photo:** The Granger Collection (t); Penta Springs Limited (cl). **28 Alamy Stock Photo:** Niday Picture Library (b). **29 Alamy Stock Photo:** Granger Historical Picture Archive (tl). **Getty Images:** Gado (tr); Print Collector (b). **30 Getty Images:** Bettmann (tr); Interim Archives (b). **31 Getty Images:** Archive Photos (b); Hulton Archive (t). **32 Alamy Stock Photo:** Gem Archive. **33 Alamy Stock Photo:** The Picture Art Collection (t). **Beinecke Rare Book and Manuscript Library, Yale University:** Yale Collection of Western Americana (b). **34 Alamy Stock Photo:** DBHC 7 (bl); Science History Images (t). **35 Alamy Stock Photo:** Associated Press (c). **Getty Images:** Fotosearch (bl); Universal History Archive (tl). **36 Alamy Stock Photo:** North Wind Picture Archives (bl). **Getty Images:** duncan1890 (tr). **37 Alamy Stock Photo:** Heritage Image Partnership Ltd (tr). **Bancroft Library, University of California Berkeley. Shutterstock.com:** Morphart Creation (bl). **38 Alamy Stock Photo:** Niday Picture Library (bl); Wirestock, Inc. (br). **39 Getty Images:** Historical (t); Stock Montage (b). **40 Bancroft Library, University of California Berkeley:** (b). **41 Alamy Stock Photo:** Michael DeFreitas North America (t). **43 Alamy Stock Photo:** Science History Images.

Cover images: *Front:* **Alamy Stock Photo:** Classic Image c, FLHC 21 br; **Shutterstock.com:** optimarc bl, pamas t/ (background); *Back:* **Alamy Stock Photo:** North Wind Picture Archives t, Ian Paterson c; **Getty Images:** Hulton Archive b.

All the books in the DK Super History series have been reviewed by authenticity readers to ensure the represented cultures and experiences are accurate.

This book uses language as appropriate to modern contexts. Historical terms that are no longer acceptable may be present in original source materials and images. These sources are included to present authentic insights into history.